ADVENTURE TIME Volume Ten, **November 2016.** Published by Titan Comics, a division of Titan Publishing Group Ltd., 144 Southwark St., London, SE1
ADVENTURE TIME, CARTOON NETWORK, the logos, and all related characters and elements are trademarks of and © Cartoon Network. (S16) Originally publish
single comic form as ADVENTURE TIME No. 45-49. © Cartoon Network. (S16) All rights reserved. All characters, events, and institutions depicted herein are fictiona
similarity between any of the names, characters, persons, events, and/or institutions in this publication to actual names, characters, and persons, whether living or
events, and/or institutions is unintended and purely coincidental.

A CIP catalog record of this book is available from The British Library.

Printed in China.

10 9 8 7 6 5 4 3 2 1

ISBN: 9781785859243

www.titan-comics.com

CREATED BY
Pendleton Ward

WRITTEN BY
Christopher Hastings

ILLUSTRATED BY
Zachary Sterling & Phil Murphy

ISSUE #45 COLORS BY
Chrystin Garland

ISSUE #46-49 COLORS BY
Maarta Laiho

ISSUES #45-48 LETTERS BY
Steve Wands

ISSUE #49 LETTERS BY
Warren Montgomery

COVER BY
Chris Houghton
COLORS BY **KASSANDRA HELLER**

With special thanks to
Marisa Marionakis, Rick Blanco, Jim Valeri, Curtis Lelash, Conrad
Montgomery, Meghan Bradley, Kelly Crews, Scott Malchus, Adam Muto
and the wonderful folks at Cartoon Network.

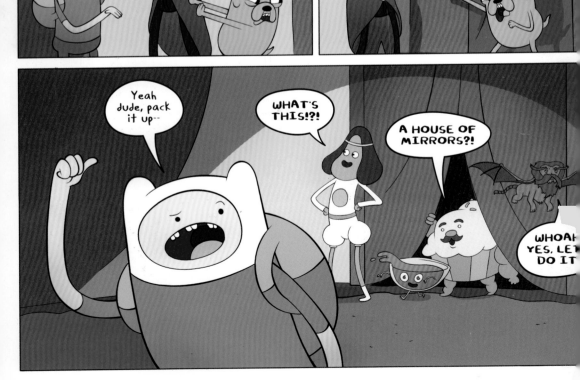

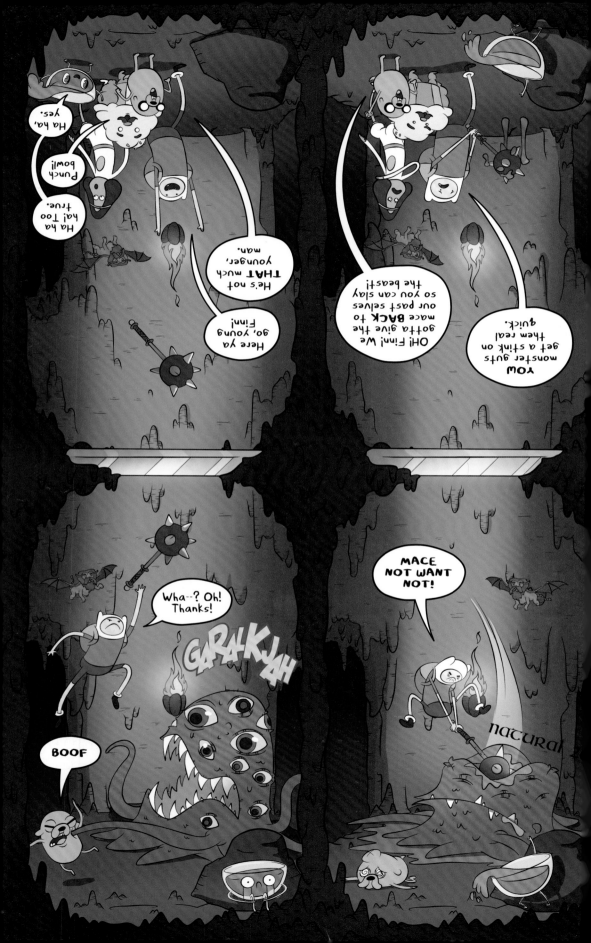

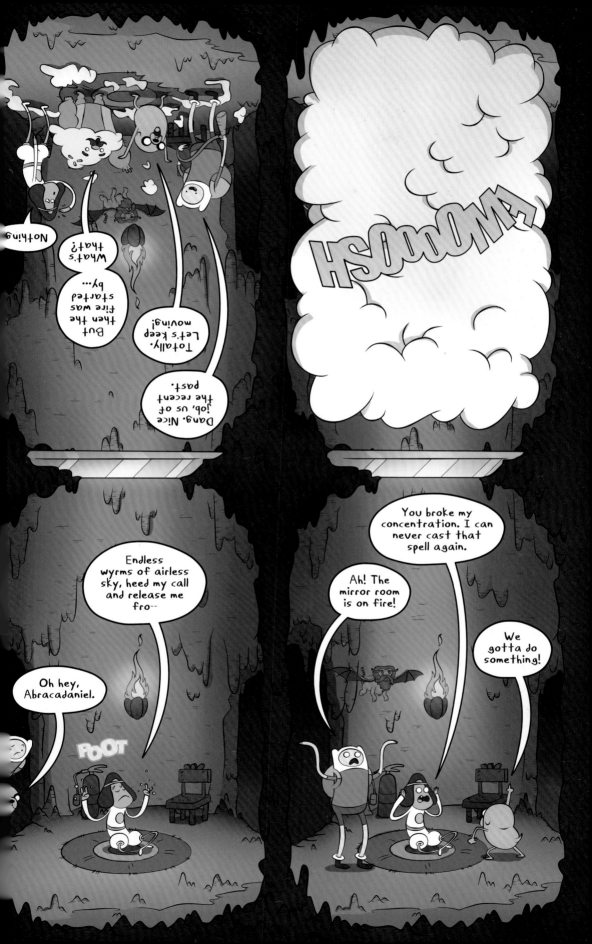

After leaving the illusionary staircase, you'll have to traverse a pit of teeth. It's real gross!

Hmm...if we'[re] supposed to pr[otect] this statue, m[oving] it out from u[nder] crumbly ceiling [is] probably a g[ood] idea.

Yeah. Hey look! Found the "intruder", heh.

Get outta here, mushrooms! You scared my holo-dad!

INTRUDER DEFEATED
hee hee hee

GAAAAAASP

KSPLASH

Aw, there you go. Little bit of sunshine will clear those shiitakes outta ya!

Ooh! Man I know I was just **CRAZY GROSS MUSHROOM INFECTED** but...

You say shiita and I'm thinkin' p Let's get a mush pizza on the w home!

Yuck, dude!

...

Okay yeah, no that sounds good.

Dude, I feel pretty bad we flubbed up Papa's mission so bad.

We were asked to do the **EXACT OPPOSITE** of what happened.

PPPFffft whatevs, bro.

I know he would have preferred you got saved instead of the statue. He's got old stuff like that everywhere. They can't all still be dangerous.

Are you sure?

HOLY BALONIES, FINN! NO WAY! STATUES FIRST! LEAVE YOUR BROTHER TO LIVE THE REST OF HIS LIFE AS A MUSH-ROOM!

He he he

h ha

Ha...

Uh...

LITERAL PIZZA VILLAGE

Hey guys. Find out what was setting off your dad's alarm?

Uh...can we...help you?

Ha ha, YEAH you can help me move some of that PIZZA into my CRUNCHBOX!

WHOAH WHOAH WHOAH

Lady, we are not accustomed to serving INTRUDERS our PIZZA.

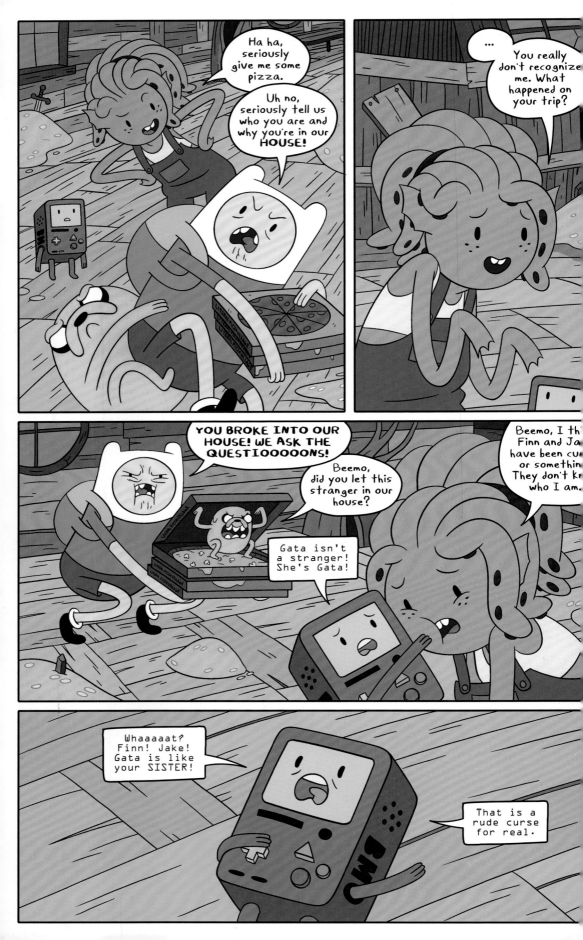

Our...

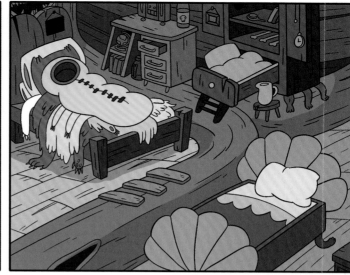

HIGH SCORES
1. 4,000 GAT
2. 3,000 GAT
3. 2,000 FIN
4. 1,000 GAT
5. 9,999 JAK

BMO

...sister?

FINN & JAKE & GATA

12
3
6

TIMELESS

aaaaaa

You're all up early!

Oh, just another thought-demon infestation that grew out of control.

Just ANOTHER? We've never fought these things before.

But--

Yeah, memory problems. They don't remember me at all either.

Excuse me!

My Ultra Mecha Suit is low on energy!

I have to charge it at my...

NUCLEAR POWER STATION!

Okay.

We know.

Later, Beemo.

You have a...

...NUCLEAR POWER STATION?

Yeah, Gata built it...you don't remember?

Byyyyyyeeeeeeeeee

But you remember us? This isn't another Mnemonoid situation, wiping years from your recollection?

No! No, we both remember everything else.

It's just THIS lady, and the uh...thought monsters. What's THEIR deal?

Gosh... they're just a constant pest.

They broadcast your inner thoughts!

I WISH I-I-I COULD TELL H-H-HER—

SQUARSH

It's annoying.

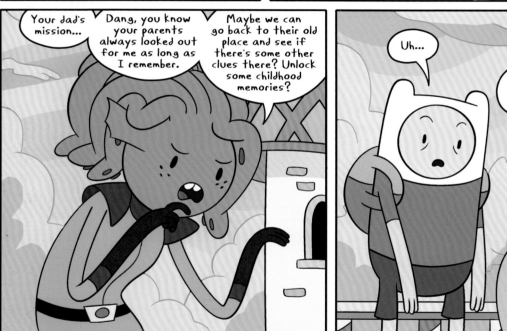

Ohh...no. Not that **HOUSE**.

The place they lived **BEFORE** you were born.

"In the old city."

We should be able to get ere by sometime tomorrow.

You remember any of this, Jake? You were born in that city!

Naaaah, not really...

NO WAIT! I DO!

Uh...I think we forgot matches.

Aaah! I'm still **CRANKY** about my wonked out memory!

And I was counting on **S'MORES** to **STOP IT.**

mm... there ight...

♪

If she can whistle that tree on fire, I'm gonna be real impressed.

FFWWPT

FWOOOOSH

AWESOME
AWESOME
AWESOME

And there we go--

Finn?

Do you... wanna...hang out or...

HA! No crushing, dork!

I like... GREW UP WITH you.

Oof!

Ha ha

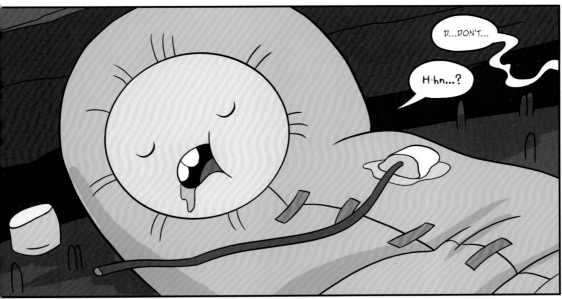

D...DON'T...

H-hn...?

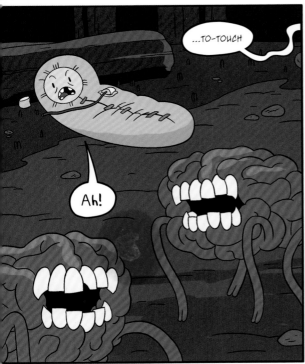

...TO-TOUCH

Ah!

MYYYYY

Jake!?

Ga--

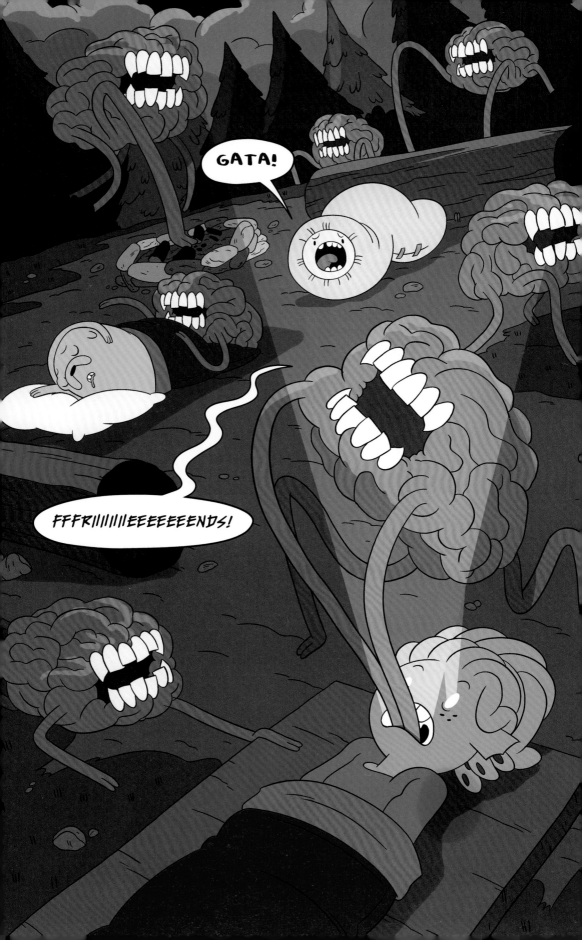

Aw, Joshua's upset because he doesn't have his hat! Here you go, big guy!

Hrlmph!

Sweet mama's multiverse! These alternate visions of reality sure don't get boring!

Sorry bout the leash, pal! There but for the grace of Glob go I!

...probably. Just have to run a FEW more EXPERIMENTS on this mysterious goop!

And hey, what's this? The boys better not be coming down here, leaving their toys!

They also shouldn't be playing with heavy faceless statues! Those make terrible toys!

This might not be the safest home in Ooo for a family...

I'm back!

Good! I don't like those freaky caves!

I don't suppose either of you boys recognize this? I found it where you should **NOT** be playing!

I didn't think you would, Jermaine. You're a very responsible and respectable baby.

And what about you, Ja--

Yipe!

It's a baby! Poor thing climbed in the window!

Looks like a **MONSTER** to me! Tell you what, we'll be fair.

Put the monster in a box. Fill the rest of the box up with apples. Put the box outside.

Monste can't eat kids. Mons gets to e apples. Ap cover prote monster f other mons Win win win--

Ah! Jake! No!

EVERYONE NEEDS TO STOP PUTTING JERMAINE IN THEIR MOUTHS!

That's right kids, you listen to Poppy!

Hm...maybe that's just what this abandoned little thing needs...

A nice Poppy?

Oh no...

Of all the dumb demons, messy monsters, weirdo witches, strange spells and unspeakable horrors...

I still haven't--

F-F-FIGURED YOU OUUUUUT

Ah! But the door was locked!

H-H-HOW'D YOU GET IN HERE

Quiet, you! The kids are in bed!

And I don't like you stealing my thoughts!

Both are bad!

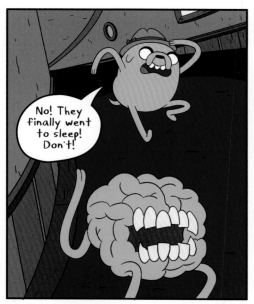

No! They finally went to sleep! Don't!

No! Not in--

--What the ding dang devil!?

GET--

--GET OUT OF THERE

Nobody told me parenting is just one long marathon of keeping gross stuff out of their mouths.

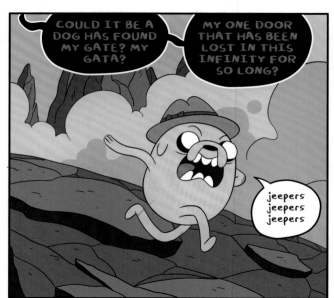

You're telling me our sweet Gata is responsible for those thought-demons?

Well, I wouldn't say that but...

Yes. They've been coming out of her mouth when she's asleep.

Baby, we moved out to the country with two nice boys, a boom boom human, and a sweet girl who's a wide open portal to a horror realm.

How did we never see it...

Maybe it's just when she snores...

I'm hungry now!

MONSTERS!

Finn!

MP

SM ASH

Oh Gata, I am sorry...

SMASH

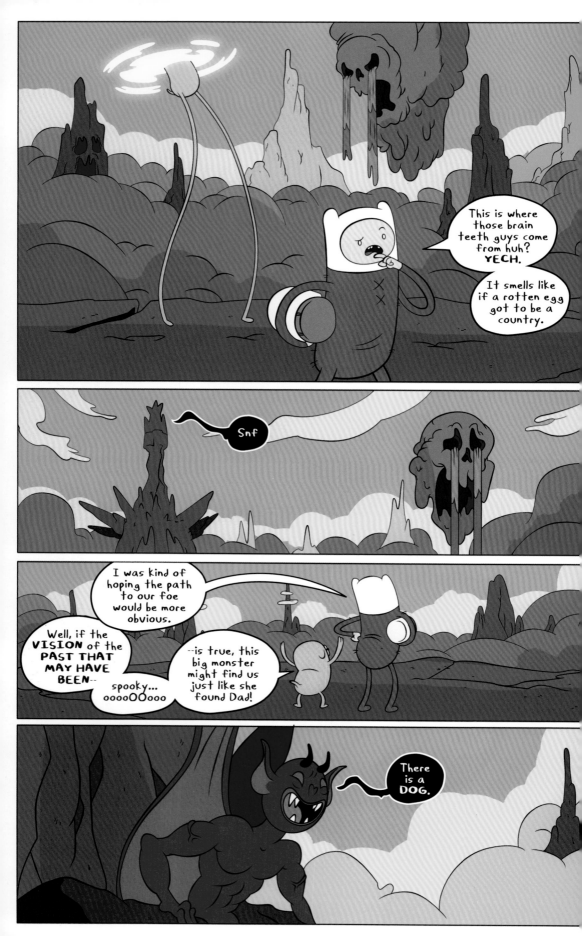

FRIEND!

Eh? Gata, I don't need the portal open now.

We think you do!

AH!

FWOOOMP

Ha ha! Yes! Put Mommy back in the bottle!

It won't last.

I've finally found my Gata and I can return any time I please--

Issue 45 Cover:
Jason Ho

Issue 46 Subscription Cover:
Vivian Ng

Issue 47 Cover:
Nichole Gustufsson

Issue 48 Cover:
Maya Kern

Issue 49 Cover:
Asia Kendrick-Horton

Issue 49 Subscription Cover:
K.L. Ricks